A Poetical Journey Through Sefirat HaOmer

Rabbi Dr. Steven Moss

Albion
Andalus
Boulder, Colorado
2021

*"The old shall be renewed,
and the new shall be made holy."*

— Rabbi Avraham Yitzhak Kook

Albion-Andalus, Inc.
P. O. Box 19852
Boulder, CO 80308
www.albionandalus.com

Cover design by Daryl McCool
Design and layout by Albion-Andalus Books

ISBN-13: 978-1-953220-07-3

Printed in the United States of America

Praise for *A Poetical Journey Through Sefirat HaOmer*

"Putting the music of the *sefiros* to poetry is a great challenge to the heart and mind, as well as the soul. But Rabbi Moss has been able to dig deep within all three to produce these beautiful poems. Readers will hopefully learn how to take the journey."

— Rabbi Tuvia Teldon, Director, Chabad Long Island

"Rabbi Steven Moss has created a poetic travelogue in an elegant and accessible way. The mystical journey that *Sefirat HaOmer* embodies can serve as a daily meditation or as an inspirational exercise as the mood strikes. Both contemporary and traditional, the reader will be drawn to the beautiful poetry and enjoy the sublime wisdom of the generations. A book of rare beauty, written by a highly respected and beloved rabbinic mentor. Thoughts of the Omer will hold a special place for both the casual as well as knowledgeable student to be read and loved. I enthusiastically recommend this lovely work for everyone."

— Rabbi Raphael Adler, Temple Anshei Shalom, Delray Beach, Florida

"Rabbi Steven Moss has succeeded in breathing new life into an ancient practice. Through the use of poetry and personal reflection, he brings to modern eyes a new sense for how to mark the sacred time between Passover and Shavuot. Anyone who is interested in doing a deeper exploration of Jewish spiritual wisdom would do well to engage in the work that he has laid out."

— Rabbi Anthony Fratello, Shaarei Shalom

"Steve Moss has written a hypnotic series of poems to enhance our spiritual experience during the Counting of the Omer. His tools are the kabbalistic *sephirot,* which he juxtaposes, two at a time, according to the tradition. Thus, we meditate upon, for example, *Hesed* in *Hesed; Gervurah* in *Hesed; Tiferet* in *Hesed.* If this seems daunting, fear not. Rabbi Moss provides a guide to this use of the terminology in his introduction, and, in any event, the rhythm of his use of these terms becomes clear as the reader progresses through them.

"These are deeply felt love poems to the many aspects of God and of the man or woman who longs to experience flakes of the Divine according to the interwoven meanings of the word pairs under poetic exploration. Each poem is a meditation, which draws us inward and upward. At the same time, they all cast their spell upon the reader, inviting us to enter into a different and spiritual realm as we move ourselves from Pesach to Shavuot, from redemption to revelation, while inviting us to a recreation of our own individual consciousness."

— Rabbi Philip Cohen

My words of thank you come from my heart,
In truth I am not sure even where to start
But let me begin by thanking my wife Judy, my dear,
For the love and support she gives me throughout the year.
I must express gratitude to my great grandfather
*   Reb Zev Turbovitz,*
I pray that my poems are all he could ever wish.
And then a thank you to my teacher Rabbi Eliyahu Shear
Whom I hold so very precious and dear,
For his teachings in Kabbalah inspire me every day
And have influenced me in so many a way.
And finally, my sincerest thanks to HaShem for
*   blessing me*
With these poems that I pray that all will see
That Sefirath HaOmer holds for us a special path indeed
That presents to the soul a delight upon which to feed,
To touch and be touched by HaShem in so many ways,
Yes, each of these holy and glorious 49 days.

CONTENTS

Preface

In 2019, I began a spiritual odyssey that opened my soul to a journey through the Sefirot that move through the 49 days between the 2nd day of Passover until the festival of Shavuot using the Mitzvah of Sefirat HaOmer, the Counting of the Omer. This Mitzvah has its roots in Leviticus chapter 23, verse 15, where it states: "From the day after the Sabbath, the day you brought the sheaf of the wave offering, count off seven full weeks". The following 49 poems reflect that journey, and it is my hope that as you read them, these poems will inspire you to go on your own journey as well.

The Mitzvah of the Counting of the Omer, Sefirat HaOmer, is observed during the 49 days that precede the festival of Shavuot, that is then the 50th day. Shavuot occurs on the sixth day of the Hebrew month of Sivan, usually in late May or early June. It commemorates the anniversary of the day G-d gave the Torah to the entire Israelite nation assembled at Mount Sinai, and the Israelites made an oath of acceptance of the Torah for their lives. Shavuot, which means either oaths or weeks, also marks the end of the 7 weeks, totally 50 days, (that includes the festival of Shavuot as the 50th day).

An Omer was a sacrifice offered in the Temple in Jerusalem on the second day of Passover, containing an omer-measure of barley. After the destruction of the 2nd Temple in 70 C.E., there was no longer any holy place where this offering could be made. The rabbis, however, created a ritual, based upon Leviticus 23:15, which would memorialize this act by the counting of the Omer each of these 49 days. Later, the students and practitioners of Kabbalah added a spiritual dimension to this ritual by utilizing the seven lower Sefirot and associating each Sefirah with a week and a day of the week.

In the schema of existence, as envisioned by the students of the Kabbalah tradition, all existence could be schematically described by what is called the Tree of Life, Etz Hayim. This Tree is constructed of 10 Sefirot (plural of Sephira). Keter, Hochmah, Binah, Hesed, Gevurah, Tiferet, Netzach, Hod, Yesod and Malchut. "A Sephira is in a way a 'filter' which transforms this light {the light of God} in a particular force or attribute by which the Creator guides the world."1 Each Sefirah is a filter of Divine energy, as expressed through Divine light, that relates to the spiritual and physical worlds and dimensions.

Keter is the highest of the Sefirot and is the one that filters the Divine light at its most intense point. Hochmah is the filter of Divine light of wisdom or pure thought. Binah is the filter of understanding that arises after reflecting back on Hochmah. These first three Sefirot are thickly veiled from the remaining Sefirot and therefore are not a part of the meditations used during the 49 days of the counting of the Omer.

The counting begins with Hesed that is the filter of Divine light of unconditional love and kindness. Gevurah is the filter of Divine light that is restrictive of the emotions that flow limitlessly from Hesed. Tiferet is the filter that balances the previous two Sefirot and therefore is the filter of harmony and peace. Hod is the filter of limitless physical energy while Netzach is the filter of limited and restricted energy. Yesod is the filter that begins the process of self-reflection and individualized identity. It is that filter of Divine light which passes the energy from the Sefirot above into Malchut—so that Malchut can be that recipient of that energy and turn it into something greater. Malchut not only receives the densest Divine energy that is experienced in our world and dimension of existence, but it is the recipient of all energy. With that energy,

Malchut will be able to achieve a new whole that is greater than simply the sum of the individual parts.

During the counting of the week, each week is under the directed flow of Divine energy of the seven Sefirot beginning with Hesed and concluding with Malchut. Each day of the week is also under the influence of a Sefirah beginning with Hesed and concluding with Malchut. This begins on Sunday with Hesed and concludes with Malchut on the Sabbath day. Each day, there is the interaction of one of the seven Sefirot and the week in which it occurs.

As an example, the first week is governed by Hesed and the first day of that week is governed by Hesed. That day is, therefore, under the Divine flow of energy brought on by the interaction between Hesed in Hesed. The second day of that week would then be Gevurah in Hesed.

On some of these 49 days, I would first pray and meditate and then write the poem. On other days, the poem would simply come to me, and I would just sit down and write it out, allowing the words from the Infinite One to flow through me.

I hope you, the reader, will enjoy the poems. They can be read any day or days of the year, but they can hold special meaning if read on their designated days of the Sefirat HaOmer. When read this second way, they can then become a part of your own counting of the Omer and your own prayers and reflections on the special meaning of these holy days that allow one to climb the 49 steps of the Sefirat HaOmer toward understanding the Divine.

As the festival of Shavuot observes the receiving of the Torah at Mt. Sinai, I might envision there being 49 steps up that mountain to the spot of Divine revelation. With each day, therefore, there is an ascent higher and ever higher. I ask you to place your hand in mine and let us climb these steps together through the words and images of the poems that I am about to share with you.

— RABBI DR. STEVEN MOSS
    March 30th, 2021

"Before reading the ten divine commands,
Let me speak in awe two words,
or three of the One who wrought the world
And sustained it since time's beginning.
At God's command is infinite power
Which words cannot define
Were all the skies parchment,
And all the reeds pens, and all the oceans ink,
And all who dwell on earth scribes,
God's grandeur could not be told."

— *Akdamut*

MEDITATIONS ON THE 49 DAYS

Week 1 – Hesed

Day 1 – Hesed in Hesed

Oh love that loves all from the All
That embraces every thing and one
From the infinite to the finite
In a hug that is so enrapturing
That it takes the breath away
And then in simultaneity gives it back
Again with a sweetness that effuses
Each petal on the Tree of Life.
Oh Hesed in Hesed if only You
Could remain, but sadly or whatever,
The march of the days must commence
And so too does life go on and on and on.

Day 2 – Gevurah in Hesed

If Hesed is to rise out of the darkness
That comes out of the arms of Gevurah
That chokes the very air which it tries
*   to breathe*
Then something needs to be done but
*   from where?*
Will it come above from the Mind that
*   speaks all*
Or rise up from the intentions of us, those
Who strive in holiness to make all that
*   is holy?*

Day 3 – Tiferet in Hesed

*If Hesed is kindness and love that
    is unending
And Tiferet is peaceful harmony
    uniting all
Then when they are together there
    is a special
Plane of existence that makes life
    worth living
Doing loving thinking feeling
    eating breathing and being.*

Day 4 – Netzach in Hesed

When Netzach is in Hesed as it is today
There is only one true thing to say
That God's life energy will not end
Except if people frivolously it do spend
The task then is to take this energy
And turn it into the power that was
Given before time itself, the big bang
If you wish, that blew open the kindness
And love that now abound beyond all
Boundaries in an every present and
Always to be flow of love that is great
In its immensity and tremendous in
Its unquestioning of who or what shall
Receive its strength now and forevermore?

Day 5 – Hod in Hesed

An energy that like a stallion wants
*   to run*
Is the Hesed that moves forward at
*   incredible*
Speeds surely beyond even the speed
*   of light*
But on this day Hod says wait wait wait
For such unbridled speed of energy
*   will destroy*
All that It wants to create and sustain.
So a balance must be held between that
Which moves forward and that
*   which holds*
The forward back into its place.

Day 6 – Yesod in Hesed

I stand looking into Yesod as I would look
    into a mirror
And at least on this day I see Hesed shining
    like a
Sun so brightly in me a sun that will never
    go out.
I stand looking into Yesod and I look deep
    into my soul
And I see a goodness that is holographically
    in every human
Being that when explored and freed can
    implode like some
Great nova bursting forth so brilliant the
    image I see bursts into
6 billion parts and maybe even more than
    tongue can tell.

Day 7 – Malchut in Hesed

With Malchut in Hesed this first week is
  ended but es
Is it just another beginning like the circle
  that just
Goes round and round no beginning and
  no end?
So here I am moving forward to the
  next week
Leaving with no feeling or sensation
  of difference
But wait it is - for Gevurah is about
  to settle in
With all it will hold back and never allow
  to flourish;
Oh stay Hesed please do not leave, let this
  first of seven
Remain forever forever forever forever and
  forever more.

Week 2 – Gevurah

Day 1 – Hesed in Gevurah

Scratched into the forehead of Hesed
*   is fear*
Fear that she will be choked, or beaten,
*   or starved*
Or locked away in some place of darkness
As Gevurah ascends into this week
*   and will*
Have its good old time of life itself;
Hesed holds on to Malchut of Hesed
And it is this rope with the upper plane
That gives it a hope that it will not die
But continue on in its mission that cannot
Ever be ended or even worse killed;
This is its lifeline, its hold onto the past
As its moves alone into the future.

Day 2 – Gevurah in Gevurah

This day is constrictive or maybe restrictive
Like the matzoh (recently eaten) it is
 binding, tying us up;
The air is tight around our necks and we
Wonder where the next breath will come
But Gevurah in Gevurah does play its part
In the process that God has placed us in
For we cannot be open all of the time
But must pull back/pull in to see the next
Step to be taken clearly and to move
 forward
Into the days and weeks ahead; so Gevurah
Do your thing and hold my breath if
 you will
For Tomorrow I will breathe again

Day 3 – Tiferet in Gevurah

At first I seem to be pulled this way
  and that
From loving to withholding from closed
  to open
From giving to keeping from shackled
  to free
Back and forth like a rope in the game
  tug of war;
But now as I am held within the grip
  of Gevurah
I can only go so far one way and
  no farther...
but even now I can bring a loosening
  to the vice
That is strangling so that it only
  strangles me
A little less than it might want to do today
And to this I say thank God.

Day 4 – Netzach in Gevurah

Unbridled judgement un-reined today
Rides in every direction causing each
One to watch and be careful knowing
That the all-seeing eye has complete
power over what is and what will be
at least for the hours of one day on a clock.

Day 5 – Hod in Gevurah

Chains are back on, the reins are ready
To be pulled back to stop the horse
From galloping away forever
As judgment is held in check
So that mercy and compassion
Can have their place in the lives
Of every person who lives
And will live by the will
Of God that needs Gevurah
But only to its boundaries
That were set in a place
That we cannot ever know.

Day 6 – Yesod in Gevurah

Looking back on this week past
The negative force of Gevurah could
*   not last;*
It had to be put into its proper place
In order for Tiferet to find its space
To bring all that has transpired to where
*   it belongs*
So let's hear Tiferet's peaceful and
*   beautiful song.*

Day 7 – Malchut in Gevurah

With the end of Gevurah and its
Vice like grip upon us we can now
Look toward Tiferet... a place of
Great peace with gardens and with streams
That flow forever without even a ripple
Upon their surface for all is in peaceful
Harmony as it flows through the
Next week's sefirot of days....

Week 3 – Tiferet

Day 1 – Hesed in Tiferet

O Tiferet rise in stead
to the hearts of men and women you
will be wed
And peace then will reign throughout
the world at last
And vile hatred will be but something
of the past.

Day 2 – Gevurah in Tiferet

It is Tiferet that best can tame Gevurah
It can unharden the hardened heart
Soften the most stubborn temper
Free the most closed of minds
Break the bonds that tie the bigot
Change the mind of hate to the soul love
For peace is the antidote for all
That prevents us from being open
To the vastness of life's universe
That is there before each of us.
So go to Tiferet Gevurah
And enjoy what is there for you.

Day 3 – Tiferet in Tiferet

As breath comes in and the next breath
　　goes out
An extra ordinary peace overwhelms
My soul as this day wraps me in a beauty
That shines throughout me into the ether
Of the Infinite and back again letting
Me ride for ever in a stream of unfettered
Consciousness that brings me into
　　the One
That is All within the All that is endless
Beyond what we know—
　　an end to everything
But in truth no end at all but a beginning.

Day 4 – Netzach in Tiferet

If Tiferet could go on forever
Unencumbered unfettered
Unrestrained unbound
To be an infinite experience
All to itself with no limits
Not one not even one
Then Tiferet would be Mashiach
And all would be in a harmony
So glorious and pristine for there
Could be no more than just this
Very experience unto itself
By itself within itself... itself!!!

Day 5 – Hod in Tiferet

Even peace itself a peace
So pure it is without any stain
Of hate, or strife, or evil
Has to have limits,
At least that is the way it seems
Until the end game
The end of time itself
When all will be engulfed
In an apocalyptic dream
That in one brief second,
Which in truth is no second at all
Since seconds then will stop
Meaning anything at all,
Will then become reality
And Mashiach will arrive
And all will just be
Forever just be.... Peace!

Day 6 – Yesod in Tiferet

When peace and harmony
Look back upon themselves
I doubt they are surprised
By what they see in the
Mirror image of their being
But rather they have to look
And be pleased beyond any
Pleasing that can be imagined
For nothing can be only that...
Pleasing... like the odor
Of the incense which was
So pleasing to the Lord...
He too had to smile as does
Tiferet now do the same.

Day 7 – Malchut in Tiferet

I can take Tiferet
That ray of hope
That lighthouse of peace
And like a precious love note
Put it in my pocket
Then in some special place
Maybe even in the closet of my heart
Looking forward to the day
When it will come out again
And shine light upon all
That brilliant light—of peace!

Week 4 – Netzach

Day 1 – Hesed in Netzach

Kindness without limits
Goodness without end
How incredible our world would be
For every one would care for every one
Else and no one would be lacking
Of love, want, or need.
If this day never ended than truly
Mashiach would be here
And an eternality of God's
Presence would be manifest
Without any question and
Without doubt.... Amen. Selah.

Day 2 – Gevurah in Netzach

Judgment can be so harsh when nothing
can stand in its way
And so too can the critical mind fail to see
the circumstances
That form the opinions and actions of
others. This then is a day
When caution must be one's banner and
to be aware that
The restrictive universe reigns
and all else will fall under its weight.

Day 3 – Tiferet in Netzach

*Time space life souls all move forward
    together
With an entropy that has enough energy
    to last
Into the infinite sequence of numbers
    without end
All being wrapped within itself in
    one perfect
Unbelievably pure and perfect harmony
That seems as if it will never ever
    come undone.*

Day 4 - Netzach in Netzach

All is moving forward not in spurts
But a free flowing forth that
Progresses with such force
Nothing can stop it as the universe
Is moving always and now past and
Into a future unbounded going
On and on with energy that will not end.

Day 5 -Hod in Netzach

Tension pushes then pulls
And then back again
Energy released with power
Untamed untouchable
Then all that power is brought
Back in again like a huge suction
Hose which then is caped to
The point inside of explosion
So that the tension now waits
To be released and it will
As the time goes by and says
NOW!

Day 6 – Yesod in Netzach

*"Turning and turning in the
  widening gyre"*
The energy of this week is ever
Widening in its output only to come
To a point of such great and awesome
Strength that it begins turning back
Into itself a process that will continue
*To infinity if it were not for this time
  this day*
When the process views itself and stops
In anticipation of the day soon to come
When all stops, even gyres, in order
To replenish itself for the next week to be.

Day 7 – Malchut in Netzach

This week is over - energy is in its place
Driving the universe – that is my life
In the direction it needs to go
For I am travelling with the spirit
    of HaShem
To a point I do not know or maybe I
Am just travelling to next week that
Begins tonight.....

Week 5 – Hod

Day 1 – Hesed in Hod

There is an energy pulsing through me
My mind, arteries, veins, heart, and soul
That is moving ever closer to a Divine
Presence that will be felt in every fiber
Of my being in the moment that is present
In the life that is this now being lived.
So I welcome this time in Hod
That is taking energy and pulling it in
Into its black hole existence so that
With the next week it will be moved further
On its path to infinity within the finite.

Day 2 – Gevurah in Hod

Everything is withheld
All is held back
Tighter than the tightest
Compressed into itself
Nothing can move forward
Not a speck on an ant's back
Or a bubble meandering
Down a stream
Or a thought that wants
To turn itself into dreams
And hopes and actions.
All is stopped up and needs
A plunger to remove the
Collected soot... it will
Come I know
It will come, I know
It will come, I am sure
It will come, I hope!

Day 3 – Tiferet in Hod

The balance of energy
Not too much and not too little
Is the golden mean of life's
Movements and progressions
For it is by balance of forces
That great force is then generated
To tear apart mountains
To move a universe further
To smash an atom
To let love, shine forth!

Day 4 – Netzach in Hod

The pulsating rhythm of drums
Beats with precision as the forces
Of nature move back and forth
And then forward a little more.
All is moving like a line that
Doesn't seem to end but will
End in the end, that's the rub,
Drawing us ever forward
Moving us like a line dance
Pushing this way and that
But ever and ever forward
With no turning back.

Day 5 – Hod in Hod – L'Ag B'Omer

O Flame full of Splendor
O Light unto the world
I join my hands with yours
And with our fingers pointed upwards
As you did so long ago
I pledge all of myself to the Law
By taking up the sword and the spear
You have given me to be strong
In counsel wisdom intellect
knowledge vision faith that not
one part of my being will be void
of your Holy Presence that will bring
me before the Holy One Blessed be He
to receive the blessing to descend
from Meron and to be a light to others
who stand in the darkness waiting,
waiting for the light to come....

Day 6 – Yesod in Hod

Yesod is mystery
Yesod is foundation
Yesod is the essence of
The past moving through the present
Into a future that is known
to only the trained
Being who follows this
Path to en-light-en-ment that
Allows a splendor so very
Bright to fill the most minute
Point of existence exploding
It in an implosive act
Into the infinite to live forever
And even more but then no more.

Day 7 – Malchut in Hod

A door closes behind
A window opens in front
A path is cleared
And sky's darkness leaves.
Life is moving ahead
At a great neck speed
Which cannot be stopped
So the next week comes
And then the next....
Let it.... There it is!

Week 6 – Yesod

Day 1 – Hesed in Yesod

Nothing stands still
Stuck in mud
Going no where
For going no where
Denies the force of life
That is propelling us
Forward in time and it is;
But now is the time to
Begin looking back
Assessing from whence
We have come as we continue
To move along the time
That does not end....

Day 2 – Gevurah in Yesod

We all withhold
We all hold back
We all judge
We all have that
Side to ourselves which is
Bad evil wild unacceptable,
But when we fail to look back
At it in the mirror of soul
We then fail to confront it
And say we got you, you
Don't got us.... but when
We can let go and move on
We then find a peace of blessing
That can be ours...

Day 3 – Tiferet in Yesod

The tremors and quakes are here my dear
The question is how much ought we fear
Should we lie at night sleepless in bed
Fearing that any day we might
*   find ourselves dead*
For peace will have been torn asunder
By some one's foolish thoughtless blunder
Or should we continue to keep the faith
*   in our heart*
And know that it is from All that all
*   will start*
To turn the world aright along its path
For peace itself is the very basis
*   of the math*
That tells us that all adds up to the future
That will be filled with a peace so
*   bright and pure*
Dispelling the darkness that seems
*   to surround us now*
But will end sometime and we know
*   not how!*

Day 4 – Netzach in Yesod

*By the very energy that will burst forth
    from within
That will enable us to overcome all,
    even sin,
And make this world a beautiful place
Where each person will look into
    another's face
And see there God's presence golden
    and bright
And then all will be ok... all will be right!*

Day 5 – Hod in Yesod

The end of the days is coming closer
The energy itself is winding down
Or is it like a black hole
Winding more and more into itself
With more and more energy
Concentrated in such a tiny ball
That just one touch of it is
To touch the universe and beyond.

Day 6 – Yesod in Yesod

One's self into itself
Can be so complex
There is then no way
Out until the head like
The head of the turtle
Peaks itself out from that
Retraining shell looks
Around this way and that
And says it is time to
Begin moving again.

Day 7 – Malchut in Yesod

Time seems to stand still
At least that's what it seems
But even at those minutes,
Seconds of unceasing
Boredom, time is still moving
Moving ever forward to
That end point which is
To come, that point when
We will meet with God
And then all will begin again.

Week 7 – Malchut

Day 1 – Hesed n Malchut

Kindness love hope faith
Now reach out to us
With such force that
We must wonder if all
Is real, until we realize
That it is the presence of
The Holy One that we feel
Overwhelming us with love
And stripping us of any doubt.
And what is realized is only
Realized through the One!

Day 2 – Gevurah in Malchut

Dissecting is for me an unpleasant task
But sometimes it is necessary to
    make things last
For sometimes we need to take
    things apart
And then to make a new fresh start.
The process is a necessary part of life
It allows for healing when there is strife,
So even a day such as this one must not
    be feared
But rather as a part of God's scheme it is
    to be revered
So that the next stage of peace
    can be achieved
And the Tree itself and its actions
    can be believed.

Day 3 – Tiferet in Malchut

A peace that comes at last
In the here and now is a
Peace that will last forever
As it is this perspective that
Is brought to every movement
Every breath every moment
Turning each one into an eternity
That by definition will last forever.

Day 4 – Netzach in Malchut

I am running to the end and
Seem unable to stop
Like a bike with no brakes
Building speed going down a hill
To where – to an end, an ending
That is coming soon but that
Ending opens up a new chapter
With its glorious story still
To be written with words
That keep on pouring forth
Like a stream that will not stop
Its flow, for there is nothing to
Stop it …. Or is there?

Day 5 – Hod in Malchut

A movement forward
Received its greatest strength
When at the last moment
All is held back and then
It moves forward with such
Energy that the universe
Opens itself up in a way
That brings the past present
Into the future maybe to go
Back again in a new way or
Maybe to go forward in
Ways unknown but
All in the palm of the
Holy One that just lies ahead!

Day 6 – Yesod in Malchut

Looking back is always hard to do
Like turning back and hitting a wall.
Looking forward is to see the world
In a new way that opens one's eyes
Heart mind soul and very being
Into possibilities that were never
Thought to exist. So to this day I
Leave you behind and look forward
To the next and look forward to a
Better day a better week a better way.

Day 7 – Malchut in Malchut

"At God's command is infinite power
Which words cannot define
Were all the skies parchment,
And all the reeds pens, and all the
    oceans ink,
And all who dwell on earth scribes,
God's grandeur could not be told."
    — Akdamut

And yet that grandeur is told
by the angels themselves
Who hand us the miracles that touch us
    each day,
But we cannot know them until
We make an apartment for God
And welcome God into our home
Our heart our soul our every sinew
Of being that opens itself into
The un-finite of infinity through
The gifts given to us that are so precious
Words themselves cannot describe them,
But without them we would not be, for
Torah and mitzvot the gifts, that are given
For us to use and never abuse,

Hold tight and to live each and
Every day; and when this is done
With every increasing consciousness
Then Malchut will rise through the upper
Worlds and all will be united in one
Glowing ember that will explode
The same time it implodes and all
Will then praise Halleluyah and
Life and all its living will dance
And sing in a symphonic alignment
Known as Mashiach, the ever present
Future that was a fleeting past of
Teachings that will move forward
With a speed unknown capturing
That light from Yehi Ohr when
Everything began and seems to
Now end but it is just a new beginning
Starting over again and again again.
Amen amen amen amen amen amen.

APPENDIX A

Sunday	Monday	Tuesday	Wednesday	Thursday	Friday	Shabbat
9 Nisan | March 25	10 Nisan | March 26	11 Nisan | March 27	12 Nisan | March 28	13 Nisan | March 29 *Bedikat Chametz*	14 Nisan | March 30 *Erev Pesach* *First Seder*	15 Nisan | March 31 *1st Day of Pesach* *Second Seder*
16 Nisan | April 1 Omer: 1 **Hesed-Hesed** *2nd Day of Pesach*	17 Nisan | April 2 Omer: 2 **Gevura-Hesed** *Interm. Day of Pesach*	18 Nisan | April 3 Omer: 3 **Tiferet-Hesed** *Interm. Day of Pesach*	19 Nisan | April 4 Omer: 4 **Netzach-Hesed** *Interm. Day of Pesach*	20 Nisan | April 5 Omer: 5 **Hod-Hesed** *Interm. Day of Pesach*	21 Nisan | April 6 Omer: 6 **Yesod-Hesed** *7th Day of Pesach*	22 Nisan | April 7 Omer: 7 **Malchut-Hesed** *8th Day of Pesach*
23 Nisan | April 8 Omer: 8 **Hesed-Gevura**	24 Nisan | April 9 Omer: 9 **Gevura-Gevura**	25 Nisan | April 10 Omer: 10 **Tiferet-Gevura**	26 Nisan | April 11 Omer: 11 **Netzach-Gevura**	27 Nisan | April 12 Omer: 12 **Hod-Gevura** *Yom Ha-shoah*	28 Nisan | April 13 Omer: 13 **Yesod-Gevura**	29 Nisan | April 14 Omer: 14 **Malchut-Gevura** *Shemini*
30 Nisan | April 15 Omer: 15 **Hesed-Tiferet** *Rosh Chodesh*	1 Iyar | April 16 Omer: 16 **Gevura-Tiferet** *Rosh Chodesh*	2 Iyar | April 17 Omer: 17 **Tiferet-Tiferet**	3 Iyar | April 18 Omer: 18 **Netzach-Tiferet** *Yom HaZikaron*	4 Iyar | April 19 Omer: 19 **Hod-Tiferet** *Yom Ha'Atzma'ut*	5 Iyar | April 20 Omer: 20 **Yesod-Tiferet**	6 Iyar | April 21 Omer: 21 **Malchut-Tiferet** *Tazria-Metzora*
7 Iyar | April 22 Omer: 22 **Hesed-Netzach**	8 Iyar | April 23 Omer: 23 **Gevura-Netzach**	9 Iyar | April 24 Omer: 24 **Tiferet-Netzach**	10 Iyar | April 25 Omer: 25 **Netzach-Netzach**	11 Iyar | April 26 Omer: 26 **Hod-Netzach**	12 Iyar | April 27 Omer: 27 **Yesod-Netzach**	13 Iyar | April 28 Omer: 28 **Malchut-Netzach** *Achrei Mot- Kedoshim*
14 Iyar | April 29 Omer: 29 **Hesed-Hod**	15 Iyar | April 30 Omer: 30 **Gevura-Hod**	16 Iyar | May 1 Omer: 31 **Tiferet-Hod**	17 Iyar | May 2 Omer: 32 **Netzach-Hod**	18 Iyar | May 3 Omer: 33 **Hod-Hod** *Lag B'Omer*	19 Iyar | May 4 Omer: 34 **Yesod-Hod**	20 Iyar | May 5 Omer: 35 **Malchut-Hod** *Emor*
21 Iyar | May 6 Omer: 36 **Hesed-Yesod**	22 Iyar | May 7 Omer: 37 **Gevura-Yesod**	23 Iyar | May 8 Omer: 38 **Tiferet-Yesod**	24 Iyar | May 9 Omer: 39 **Netzach-Yesod**	25 Iyar | May 10 Omer: 40 **Hod-Yesod**	26 Iyar | May 11 Omer: 41 **Yesod-Yesod**	27 Iyar | May 12 Omer: 42 **Malchut-Yesod** *Behar-Bechukotai*
28 Iyar | May 13 Omer: 43 **Hesed-Malchut** *Yom Yerushalayim*	29 Iyar | May 14 Omer: 44 **Gevura-Malchut**	1 Sivan | May 15 Omer: 45 **Tiferet-Malchut** *Rosh Chodesh*	2 Sivan | May 16 Omer: 46 **Netzach-Malchut**	3 Sivan | May 17 Omer: 47 **Hod-Malchut**	4 Sivan | May 18 Omer: 48 **Yesod-Malchut**	5 Sivan | May 19 Omer: 49 **Malchut – Malchut** *Bamidbar* *Tikkun Leil Shavuot*
6 Sivan | May 20 *Shavuot I*	7 Sivan | May 21 *Shavuot II*	8 Sivan | May 22	9 Sivan | May 23	10 Sivan | May 24	11 Sivan | May 25	12 Sivan | May 26 *Nasso*

Shavu'ot, the holiday of the giving of the Torah, is Sunday and Monday, May 20th and 21st.
The holiday begins Saturday evening, May 19th, with an all night study session.

This *Sefirah* chart shows how the *Sefirot* interact on a weekly and daily basis. This indicates how the meditations were done according to the calendar 2018/5778.

Appendix B

Keter
כתר
Crown
Ehyeh
Ancient of Days

Binah
בינה
Understanding
YHVH Elohim
Ima

Chokkmah
חכמה
Wisdom
Yah
Abba

Da'at
דעת
Knowledge

Gevurah
גבורה
Strength, Law
Elohim
Structure

Chesed
חסד
Loving-kindness
El
Flow

Tiferet
תפארת
Beauty
YHVH
Tzaddik

Hod
הוד
Splendor
Elohim Tzvaot
Free Will

Netzach
נצח
Victory
Adonai Tzvaot
God's Will

Yesod
יסוד
Foundation
El Chai
Relationship

Malchut
מלכות
Sovereignty
Adonai
Nukva

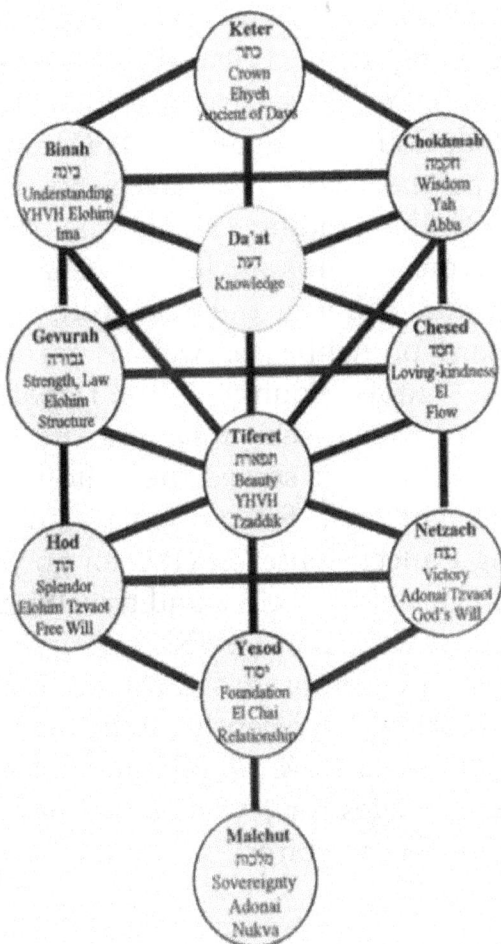

This is a diagram of the *Etz Hayyim,* Tree of Life,
showing the 10 *Sefirot*

Rabbi Dr. Steven Moss has served B'nai Israel in Oakdale, Long Island, as its Rabbi since 1972. He is now Rabbi Emeritus. He is past chairperson of the Suffolk County Human Rights Commission as well as the Center for Social Justice and Human Understanding. He is the recipient of numerous awards including Chaplain of the Year and Rabbi of the Year from the New York Board of Rabbis, as well as recognition from the Suffolk County Police Department, the County Executive's office and the District Attorney's office. He served the Suffolk County Police Department for 34 years and Sloan-Kettering Cancer Center in NYC for 30 years as chaplain. He enjoys cycling and travelling. He is a student of Kabbalah (Jewish mysticism) and has taught numerous programs on Kabbalah and meditation. He recently published a book, *God is With Me; I Have No Fear* and has written numerous articles for JewishSacredAging.com. He is a Florida snowbird.